D0938106

To my Good, no, Great Friend, Bonnie — one of the best people I know. xo, Love, Terry

FRIENDSHIP

Edited by
Tiddy Rowan

Quadrille
PUBLISHING

The meaning of friendship can vary according to the different stages of people's lives. However, there are certain key elements that always constitute a real friendship.

- It is a mutually beneficial relationship.

- There is a deep enjoyment of each other's company.

- There are demonstrations of affection and loyalty.

There are two basic things that most people want in life: to be understood and to be appreciated. A true friendship provides both.

The ancient Greek philosopher Aristotle divided friendship into three categories: kinship, utility and affection. These three categories can still be applied to modern friendships and described as familial, instrumental and useful, and emotional.

Kinship is a friendship that is an extension of family or personal connections where there is a familial tie. There is no expectation of a deeper friendship developing, but there is a sense of duty.

Utility refers to agentic friendships. This is where both parties become friends by helping each other in a common goal or work task. Personal emotions and information are not shared.

Affection is a friendship born out of mutual attraction and affection and is the highest form of friendship. Essentially it is a deep bond that develops through trust and empathy. Emotions and confidences are shared and there is a love for the other person because of who they are – not because of what they do or because of their place within the family circle.

"The crown of these
Is made of love and friendship,
*   and sits high*
Upon the forehead of humanity."

JOHN KEATS
Endymion

JOHN KEATS
Endymion

True friendships improve all aspects of our lives. They give us camaraderie, encouragement, confidence and joy. All the qualities that improve our health and bring happiness to us.

The fundamental friendship characteristics.

Empathy
Sympathy
Affection
Honesty
Ability to be oneself
Ability to express one's feelings
Truthfulness
Mutual understanding
Steadfastness
Compassion
Trust
Sincerity

Friendships form because people are instinctively drawn to each other. Be mindful of what messages you send out, as people will be attracted to your magnetism.

'Elective affinity' is a term that has come to mean the attraction between friends or lovers. It originates from the technical term describing the preferential attraction between two chemical substances and denotes the chemistry between two people. Johann Wolfgang von Goethe explored this theme in his novel *Elective Affinities* published in 1809.

"We don't get to know people when they come to us; we have to go to them so as to learn what they are like."

JOHANN WOLFGANG VON GOETHE
Elective Affinities

In 450BC, the Greek philosopher Empedocles used chemical analogies to describe friendship.

"People who love each other mix like water and wine; people who hate each other segregate like water and oil."

EMPEDOCLES

Although the chemistry of attraction might produce the alchemy of friendship, the development and safekeeping of it cannot depend on happenstance. It has to be nurtured.

Always take the opportunity to lift your friends up – encourage them, compliment them and acknowledge what they do for you.

Always behave towards your friends as you would like them to behave towards you.

"A friend is someone who gives you total freedom to be yourself."

JIM MORRISON

"However rare true love may be, it is less so than true friendship."

ALBERT EINSTEIN

With the great social changes of the 20th century came the dispersion of people who had previously stayed in family groups in rural or urban areas. There was increasing integration between the different classes as friendships between people who might have been viewed as unequals became accepted.

By the late 20th century and early 21st century, friendships of all varieties began to develop as social networks broadened and reached a zenith with Facebook. Although the concept of friendship has been transformed by the internet, there is still no substitute for the physical and emotional bonds we create with real friends.

The deluge of social media has made it easier to find friends. The word 'friend' has become a very broad term: it can cover everyone from someone you've met online; acquaintances such as someone you went to school with, and even someone who you have a friend in common with. In this ever-changing world, it is important to remember what a true friend is and what real friendship constitutes.

There is a difference between being popular on social media and being a real friend.

Having thousands of Facebook friends or Twitter or Instagram followers suggests a desire to be popular, rather than the ability of being a true and loyal friend.

In true friendships, there will be times when we have to put ourselves out for a friend, to be prepared to get up in the middle of the night in an emergency, to listen to a litany of their sorrows, or share in their celebrations and toast their successes.

"It's the friends you can call up at 4 a.m. that matter."

MARLENE DIETRICH

" *Some people go to priests; others to poetry; I to my friends.* "

VIRGINIA WOOLF
The Waves

Familiar and established relationships tend to take precedence over new ones, yet new and lasting friendships can be made at any age.

One of the greatest qualities of a true friend is that they makes us feel truly good about ourselves.

"*Friendship improves happiness, and abates misery, by doubling our joys, and dividing our grief.*"

MARCUS TULLIUS CICERO

Some friendships endure for a lifetime.
Come hell or high water.

"Friendship is the only cement that will ever hold the world together."

WOODROW WILSON

When new possibilities arise in friendships, we should be flexible and open to new adventures.

"What do you most value in your friends? Their continued existence."

CHRISTOPHER HITCHENS
Hitch-22: A Memoir

Just because we are close friends with someone doesn't mean that their feelings are invulnerable. Be honest, yet gentle with the truth.

Inevitably some friendships will unravel and not survive rapidly changing circumstances. Managing our own expectations of what it takes to keep a friendship alive helps us achieve a clearer view of how it can either evolve or dissolve.

When meeting new people, common courtesy and politeness is important, but there can be times when our over-politeness is misinterpreted as a signal to engage in a friendship. We should be aware of the signals we give off.

In business and social behaviour
it is good to recognise the distinction
between becoming a friend and simply
being friendly.

Give new friendships time to develop.

"Wishing to be friends is quick work, but friendship is a slow-ripening fruit."

ARISTOTLE

Childhood friendships play an important part in developing our interpersonal skills, as well as building the foundations of self-awareness and identity.

In the intervening period between the end of childhood and adulthood, friendships are the most important relationships in the emotional life of an adolescent and are often more intense than relationships formed later in life.

"What was more, they had taken the first step toward genuine friendship. They had exchanged vulnerabilities."

ARTHUR C. CLARKE
2010: Odyssey Two

Expectations for a 'best friend' become increasingly complex, as a child gets older. A study investigated such criteria in a sample of 480 children between the ages of six and fourteen. Their findings highlighted three stages of development in friendship expectations. In the first stage, children emphasised shared activities and the importance of geographical closeness. In the second, they emphasised sharing, loyalty and commitment. In the final stage, they increasingly desired similar attitudes, values and interests.

www.integratedsociopyschology.net

"Friends are as companions on a journey, who ought to aid each other to persevere in the road to a happier life."

PYTHAGORAS

When we leave our family home we usually gravitate towards a place or community which is familiar or where we might know people. Friendships can develop quickly at that fledgling age whilst we're finding our feet.

A study was designed to examine ongoing close friendships among same sex adults. An analysis of frequency and depth of conversational topics was undertaken. The self-reports of female participants showed that they converse more frequently than the male participants about intimate topics and daily and shared activities. Sex differences on depth of topic discussion also emerged, with females reporting greater depth in topics involving personal and family matters.

Sports were the only topic for which males, rather than females, reported both more frequent discussion and conversation in greater depth. The topic frequency were factor analyzed for each sex group. The factor analyses indicated patterns for the males on 'personal issues,' 'sociocultural issues,' and 'activity' and patterns for females on 'domestic matters,' 'personal issues,' and 'worldy issues.' The results of the study generally support sex-stereotypical assumptions about the nature of male-male and female-female friendships.

ELIZABETH J. ARIES
Close Friendship in Adulthood

"A lot of women, when they're young, feel they have very good friends, and find later on that friendship is complicated. It's easy to be friends when everyone's 18."

ZADIE SMITH

As our circumstances change, we may find ourselves having to make new friends. A divorce, separation, change of job, moving to a new home, friends moving away, all offer opportunities for potential new friendships to form in our lives.

The British anthropologist Robin Dunbar has taken an evolutionary psychological approach to the understanding of human development, which has led to the theory of 'Dunbar's number'. He theorised that there is a limit of approximately 150 people with whom a human can maintain stable social relationships.

"What does your work tell us about the way we interact socially?

We're members of the primate family – and within the primates there is a general relationship between the size of the brain and the size of the social group... there is a natural grouping of 150. This is the number of people you can have a relationship with involving trust."

www.theguardian.com
Robin Dunbar interviewed by Aleks Krotoski

Friendship increases the body's production of oxytocin, which is commonly referred to as the 'bonding hormone'.

Deep, close friendships make us feel better about ourselves, contributing to our self-esteem, confidence, sense of identity and place within society.

Good friendships enhance an individual's overall happiness and well-being.

Good friends encourage each other to lead healthier lifestyles, suggest that their friends seek help when in trouble, support their friends in dealing with illness and other health problems and boost their friends' positive mentality, all of which ultimately improves both physical and mental health.

"My best friend brings out the best in me."

HENRY FORD

Moods are infectious.

Although there are times when we feel genuinely sad or down, there are also times when it is out of laziness or selfishness that we don't want to put on a good disposition around our friends. Be mindful of how your mood effects those around you.

Words are not the only way to communicate your feelings to your friends. Facial expressions, body language, eye contact, hand gestures and mannerisms, all reflect how you are feeling, just as much as the spoken word.

Be friendly.

Engage with a friendly face and smile.

*" The smile that you
send out returns to you."*

ANCIENT INDIAN PROVERB

Practising mindfulness helps us manage our stress levels and increase our confidence. By feeling more relaxed and more self-assured, we improve our nonverbal communication, as we are able to access a more authentic and sincere place in ourselves, rather than coming from a strained and affected one.

*" The language of friendship
is not words but meanings."*

HENRY THOREAU

Think of the qualities you would like to be known for in your friendships. Then grow into them.

Qualities of being a good friend.

Be a good listener, pay attention, give animated responses and have a relaxed and open manner.

The essential characteristics of friendship can be found in the relationships humans have with their animals, as they share a sense of loyalty, mutual support, trust, reciprocity, affection and respect.

Some people develop very close attachments to pets or animals. Dogs are typically described as 'man's best friend' and there are many examples of how these friendships can replicate human friendships.

"... there is no religion without love, and people may talk as much as they like about their religion, but if it does not teach them to be good and kind to man and beast, it is all a sham..."

ANNA SEWELL
Black Beauty

Nurturing good friendships now
will make them last a lifetime.

It would be untypical to have only one friend who can provide and sustain all a person's friendship needs. Into adulthood, we make various friends who support the different aspects of our lives – work friends, social friends, intimate friends, single friends and even intellectually challenging friends.

Having a best friend – a true
and close friend – is often a pairing
that is recognised by other people.
In particular, children and
adolescents are often referred
to as being 'inseparable'.

"Constant use had not worn ragged the fabric of their friendship."

DOROTHY PARKER

A true and intimate friend is
sometimes referred to as an 'alter ego'
– in other words 'another self'.

"What is a friend? A single soul dwelling in two bodies."

ARISTOTLE

Geographical distance can prevent physical togetherness, but a test of a good friendship is when even after a length of time has passed the friendship is still as fresh and as strong as ever.

"More than kisses, letters mingle souls,
For thus friends absent speak."

JOHN DONNE
To Sir Henry Wotton

"Be slow in choosing a friend, slower in changing."

BENJAMIN FRANKLIN

A fair-weather friend is someone who only expresses friendship when circumstances are beneficial to them. But when you need them, they are unresponsive. Watch out for this behaviour – be aware that these are not reliable friends

"Lots of people want to ride with you in the limo, but what you want is someone who will take the bus with you when the limo breaks down."

OPRAH WINFREY

It is an interesting exercise to define exactly what we mean by friendship. It clarifies whether we are being 'well friend-ed' and if we are being a good friend in return.

Make a list of what you really want
and need out of your friendships.

Friendship Exercise.

Make a list of ten people you regard as being in your close circle of friends.

- Ask yourself which of these ten people would you get up out of bed for in the middle of the night?

- Which of those ten would you travel some distance to be with at a time of their need?

- Then ask yourself, for which of them would you cancel an important interview or party if their need warranted the sacrifice?

In a marriage, two people enter into a contract as a result of intimate love. However, in a friendship there are no rules, no commitments and no contracts. Friendship develops out of the simple desire to share a mutual bond and to care for a friend, only following guidelines that are instinctively arrived at.

Sharing is a component of friendship.

In friendships we share experiences, confidences, knowledge, sorrows and celebrations.

Trust is a component of friendship.

Casual friendships often overlook
some of the characteristics that
underline a deep friendship,
such as fidelity, loyalty, trust
and truthfulness.

Friendships at work do develop naturally. However, the test of these friendships comes when the workplace is no longer the foundation upon which the friendship is based.

"*Friendship is constant in all other things Save in the office and affairs of love.*"

WILLIAM SHAKESPEARE
Much Ado About Nothing

"Of all things which wisdom provides to make us entirely happy, much the greatest is the possession of friendship."

EURIPIDES

" *There is nothing I would not do for those who are really my friends. I have no notion of loving people by halves, it is not my nature.* "

JANE AUSTEN
Northanger Abbey

As we grow older, our memories still remain just as youthful. Sharing memories of good times with friends provides great pleasure.

"From quiet homes and first beginning,
Out to the undiscovered ends,
There's nothing worth the
wear of winning,
But laughter and the love of friends."

HILAIRE BELLOC
Dedicatory Ode

"It is one of the blessings of old friends that you can afford to be stupid with them."

RALPH WALDO EMERSON

"I love everything that's old: old friends, old times, old manners, old books, old wines."

OLIVER GOLDSMITH
She Stoops to Conquer

Parents, grandparents, guardians, godparents, siblings, teachers and mentors all have a role to play in guiding children through early friendships.

How to encourage a child to develop friendships.

- In the playground or at a party encourage children to watch what the other children are doing. Ask them what they think they could do to fit in.

- Encourage them to always ask to join in a game or a group.

- Tell them to smile.

- Teach them that they must behave with their friends how they would want to be treated.

"*Be who you are and say what you feel because those who mind don't matter and those who matter don't mind.*"

ANONYMOUS

Take the opportunity to offer a friendly ear whenever you can.

Be an example to your children
or siblings by managing your
own friendships meaningfully.
Emphasise the need for truthfulness
and kindness.

As children grow, their friendships become more complex and can become increasingly emotionally fraught. Their friendships evolve from the simple, shared intimacies of early childhood to the boundary testing and even cruelty that can occur in later childhood encompassing betrayal, gossip, malicious teasing and purposeful exclusion.

"When I see a fellow-creature about to perish through the cowardice of her pretended friends, I wish to be allowed to speak, that I may say what I know of her character."

MARY SHELLEY
Frankenstein

"You don't love someone for their looks, or their clothes, or for their fancy car, but because they sing a song only you can hear."

ANONYMOUS

Reflecting on how a friendship came about helps us be mindful of what it was about us that the other person was attracted to and similarly what attracted us to the friend in the first place.

"It is not a lack of love, but a lack of friendship that makes unhappy marriages."

FRIEDRICH NIETZSCHE

If time is our most precious currency –
and ours to spend as we like or
need – then what greater gift can
we offer our friends than to put time
aside for them?

Never take your friendships for granted.

It's important to keep in touch. Touch being the key word – make time to visit each of your close friends.

"A letter always seemed to me like immortality because it is the mind alone without corporeal friend."

EMILY DICKINSON

A phone call to a friend is a meaningful way of staying in touch because it involves setting aside time for them. Why not send a letter or a postcard to remind them that you're thinking of them, it's more personal than an email or a text and is a physical token of your appreciation and affection.

Unless your friendship group is localised to your area there are fewer opportunities to catch up in person with your friends. However, with close friends who don't live nearby ensure that you put the effort and time into meeting up at least once a year.

"A man should keep his friendship in constant repair."

SAMUEL JOHNSON

Giving a personal present to a friend for no reason is a double gift.

" You have not lived today until you have done something for someone who can never repay you."

JOHN BUNYAN

Whatever your age or circumstances, it's never too late to make new friends or reconnect with old ones.

Unless it's inappropriate, start a conversation with a smile. It sends positive signals to the other person and displays amicability. Practise smiling more. It's also a good exercise for the face muscles and puts you into a better frame of mind. If it doesn't come naturally, then practise in front of the mirror until it does to make sure your smile doesn't look forced.

Small talk can be daunting – especially if you think it is too light. It might seem trivial, but it is a convention for exploring other people's reactions, mannerisms, responses, level of eye contact and an exercise in establishing common ground and interest.

Small talk includes: the weather, the surroundings, mutual friends, general interests or your work.

When meeting new people, ask open questions (which invite a considered reply) rather than closed ones (which only allows a 'yes' or 'no' answer). For example, instead of saying 'Did you have a good time?' ask 'What did you enjoy about the film/party/concert?' Open-ended questions begin with who, where, when or how.

When looking to expand your friendship circle, it can be more effective to find a single-themed activity rather than a general interest one. For example, learning to play the guitar or joining a drama group will focus your shared interests quickly.

"A friend may be waiting behind a stranger's face."

MAYA ANGELOU
Letter to My Daughter

**Ways of accelerating
friendship potential.**

- Are you friendly towards your neighbours? It's sociable as well as good practice to smile at people and say hello.

- Take a class in something you wouldn't normally do.

- Change the way you holiday. Go on an adventure. There are plenty of group travel organisations. People tend to bond naturally and form friendships within a group that can endure beyond the shared holiday experience.

- Even if you shy away from the idea of joining a club, it's good to take the plunge and put yourself in a new enviroment filled with new people.

- Invite people from within your area to start a lunch or supper club. Rotate the get-togethers in each others homes and have everyone contribute something to the meal. Friendships form naturally over the informality of cooking and sharing food and drink together.

According to recent studies, when meeting someone new it takes us less than a few seconds to instinctively judge certain attributes in the other person. Keep your inner light switched on.

"*The meeting of two personalities is like the contact of two chemical substances: if there is any reaction, both are transformed.*"

CARL JUNG
Modern Man in Search of a Soul

"We sometimes encounter people, even perfect strangers, who begin to interest us at first sight, somehow suddenly, all at once, before a word has been spoken."

FYODOR DOSTOEVSKY
Crime and Punishment

You never get a second chance
to make a good first impression.

Our voices carry inflections that unbeknownst to us express our feelings – whether it's assertiveness, compassion, disappointment or sarcasm. Be mindful of your tone.

A firm handshake, a meaningful hug, a touch on the arm or cheek all convey amicability and reassurance.

"Friendship is born at that moment when one person says to another: 'What! You too? I thought I was the only one.'"

C.S. LEWIS
The Four Loves

People are understandably protective about certain friendships. If you meet a friend through a pre-existing friend and want to meet them again, it's polite to either include the friend that introduced you or to tell them that you're going to meet up.

People we don't know form judgments about us through the company we keep and the friends we have. We should be proud of our circle of friends.

When you are talking to a friend, don't be distracted by what is going on around you or the other people in a restaurant, bar or party.

" True friends stab you in the front."

OSCAR WILDE

Be truthful with friends.

Don't only tell them what you think they want to hear.

"Kindness is the language which the deaf can hear and the blind can see."

MARK TWAIN

The essence of every religion is kindness and compassion. Let kindness and compassion be our approach to all of our friendships.

"The best way I can be a friend to my friend – is to be his friend."

HENRY THOREAU

" If we would build on a sure foundation in friendship, we must love friends for their sake rather than for our own."

ELIZABETH GASKELL
The Life of Charlotte Brontë

Look for the best in people.
Everyone has a 'best' in them.

"A friend is someone who knows all about you and still loves you."

ELBERT HUBBARD

We can't be happy if we're carrying around feelings of resentment towards a friend. Much better to face up to them, forgive and move on.

If you are holding onto bad feelings in a friendship, difficult though it may be to admit, realise that you may be wrong or have misunderstood something. Don't judge too quickly – or at least until you've considered things from your friend's point of view.

Whilst it's good to air feelings over important issues, try not to raise every little grievance. Practising mindfulness helps keep irrational reactions at bay.

"Oh Great Spirit, keep me from ever judging and criticizing a man until I have walked in his moccasins for two weeks."

SIOUX INDIAN INVOCATION

Get into the habit of discussing situations that are troubling you in your friendship, but explain your feelings calmly and not combatively.

Be a good listener.

Learn to know when to speak up
and when to keep quiet in order to let
the other person speak, confide, seek
guidance or approbation.

Use humour whenever you can.

It's a way of expressing your feelings and opens up a conversation. Laughter is an expression of mutual appreciation. It also releases endorphins, which gives you both a natural high – a key ingredient in friendship.

Laughter is contagious and is another bond of friendship. Learn to walk on the sunny side of the street to keep the mood light.

Developing a sense of humour is vital in guarding against unnecessary conflicts, misunderstandings or too quickly formed judgments.

Life is all too full of serious issues and difficulties we have to overcome. So whenever the opportunity presents itself, let's look for humour and remember not to take ourselves too seriously.

"*Fan the sinking flame of hilarity with the wing of friendship; and pass the rosy wine.*"

CHARLES DICKENS
The Old Curiosity Shop

Birds of a feather flock together.

- James Fowler and Nicholas Christakis, American professors, conducted research on why we choose the friends we do. According to their research, friends resemble each other genetically and share a 'functional kinship.' Their findings support the fact that similar genes shared between friends seem to be evolving faster than other genes.

- As evidence that we are influenced by our friends' behaviour, Professor Fowler's research on Facebook friendships revealed that these strongly influence voter turn out in American elections – friends who voted also influenced others to do so.

A true friendship is when we are so at ease in each other's silence that we feel no obligation to fill it. It's a measure of how comfortable we are with that friend.

We can completely be ourselves with our friends. We don't have to wear the same armour as we do when fighting our battles at work, with family or relationships, with prospective clients or employers, with whom who we may need to negotiate, cajole or placate.

" *This above all: to thine own self be true,*
And it must follow, as the night the day,
Thou canst not then be false to any man. **"**

WILLIAM SHAKESPEARE
Hamlet

Heart comes first in friendship.

Lead from the heart first and last.

"Don't walk behind me; I may not lead. Don't walk in front of me; I may not follow. Just walk beside me and be my friend."

JEWISH CHILDREN'S SONG

Keep a friend's secrets.

Trust and loyalty are the backbone
of a strong friendship.

Honour the trust in a friendship.
Don't betray confidences.
We know when information or
shared experiences are confidential
or sensitive.

Make an effort to remember names of people who are important in your friend's lives – their parents, children, boyfriend or girlfriend.

We can't assume everyone remembers our names. If you meet people you have met before but only briefly, it's thoughtful to shake hands and give them your name and explain when you met before.

If a friend give us advice, we should consider it. It is often the most valuable and useful guidance in difficult situations and challenges.

A good friend will be genuinely interested in how you feel about life and what is happening around you. In turn, you need to be supportive without being judgemental.

"A man's friendships are one of the best measures of his worth."

CHARLES DARWIN

Every month look for a way to improve one of your friendships or rekindle an old one.

A friend who is overly possessive of you, negative or critical towards you and makes you doubt your self-worth is not a good or healthy friend.

Prolonged negative and out-of-character behaviour from a friend needs to be talked about and aired before misunderstandings arise that create barriers.

Friendships that have changed the world.

Thomas Jefferson and John Adams fell out acrimoniously when Adams was President and Jefferson was his Vice President. However, after Jefferson had served two presidential terms Adams wrote Jefferson a letter wishing him many happy years to come. Their correspondence continued for 14 years.

When Adams lay on his deathbed, troubled by the future of America, his last words were 'Thomas Jefferson survives'. In fact, Jefferson had died five hours earlier.

Friendships that have founded literary movements.

- **The Romantics:** Williams Wordsworth and Samuel Taylor Coleridge created their collective work *Lyrical Ballads* (1798).

- **The Gothic:** Mary Shelley, Lord Byron, John William Polidori and Percy Shelley spent a month together in Geneva, where Mary Shelley wrote *Frankenstein* (1818).

- **The Movement:** Philip Larkin, Kingsley Amis and John Wain were all poets in this circle.

- **The Beat Generation:** Allen Gingsberg and Jack Kerouac met and founded this cult literary genre.

Social change has been achieved through the constancy of friendships formed by mutual hopes and ideals – during women's suffrage and other feminist movements, the civil rights movement in the US and even Greenpeace.

Friendships are not confined to personal relationships.

'Comrade' is a term we recognise as meaning a friend (comrade-in-arms) who shares our ideals and is a member of the same political party or social organisations and movements. The trust held in that friendship extends to the trust they must honour in upholding the tenets of the movement itself.

Celebrate the success of your friends. Share in their excitement if they get engaged, promoted or have any form of success in their life.

"*Love is like the wild rose-briar,*
Friendship like the holly-tree—
The holly is dark when the rose-
  briar blooms,
But which will bloom most constantly?"

EMILY BRONTË
Love and Friendship

Be generous.

Once in a while, pick up the tab.

Building on the basic concept of attraction and caring, the significant characteristics of friendship evolve depending on culture, proximity and shared interests.

When trust in a friendship is broken, it is hard to repair the bond. Friendships can become embittered and friends can become adversaries, love turns to hate, trust to distrust. This is because 'deep trust' needs nourishing and cherishing.

A difference of opinion or having different personalities doesn't mean you can't sustain a friendship. It's important to respect individuality.

" The positive always defeats the negative, Courage overcomes fear, Patience overcomes anger and irritability, Love overcomes hatred."

SWAMI SIVANANDA SARASWATI
Springs of Indian Wisdom

We try to juggle too many things in our increasingly busy lives. So when our friendships reach a certain plateau, we assume that they will always remain in our lives. However, since nothing stays the same, we need to remember to nurture, look after and meaningfully check from time to time that we are not taking any friendships for granted.

"I desire you in friendship, and I will one way or other make you amends."

WILLIAM SHAKESPEARE
The Merry Wives of Windsor

A test of a friendship is when you need to resolve differences. If you manage to resolve the problem, it leads to a stronger and healthier relationship – and is in part thanks to an essentially high-quality friendship.

" *When you part from your friend, you grieve not; For that which you love most in him may be clearer in his absence, as the mountain to the climber is clearer from the plain.* "

KAHLIL GIBRAN
The Prophet

Ending a friendship.

Friendships end for many different reasons. Friends may move away and the relationship diminishes due to the distance. Sometimes divorce or relationship break-ups cause an end to friendships. At a younger age, friendships may end as a result of acceptance into new social groups. Friendships may finish as the result of an irreconcilable dispute or they may simply have run their course.
Treat endings with respect and avoid resentment and grudges.
Time to move on.

In life we cannot avoid change, we cannot avoid loss. Freedom and happiness are found in the flexibility and ease with which we face these challenges.

" Life is either a daring adventure or nothing at all."

HELEN KELLER

" I am treating you as my friend, asking you to share my present minuses in the hope that I can ask you to share my future plusses."

KATHERINE MANSFIELD

"Friendship is the hardest thing in the world to explain... But if you haven't learnt the meaning of friendship, you really haven't learnt anything."

MUHAMMAD ALI

Don't lose yourself in the friendship.
Be yourself.

"Friendship with oneself is all-important because without it one cannot be friends with anyone else in the world."

ELEANOR ROOSEVELT

Resolve to never take your friends for granted, to always make time for them in happiness and in sorrow...

...to always be ready to celebrate their triumphs and to love them for who they are.

BIBLIOGRAPHY

Books mentioned in *The Little Book of Friendship*

Angelou, Maya, *Letter to my Daughter* (Little Brown, 2012)

Aries, Elizabeth J., *Close Friendship in Adulthood: Conversational Content Between Same-Sex Friends* (Sex Roles, Vol. 9, No.12, 1983)

Austen, Jane, *Northanger Abbey* (Wordsworth Editions, 1992)

Belloc, Hilaire, *Dedicatory Ode* (Complete Verse, Pimlico, 1997)

Brontë, Emily, *Love and Friendship* (Emily Brontë: The Complete Poems, Penguin Classics, 1992)

Clarke, Arthur C., *2001: Odyssey Two* (HarperCollins, 2000)

Dickens, Charles, *The Old Curiosity Shop* (Wordsworth Editions, 1995)

Donne, John, *To Sir Henry Wotton* (John Donne: The Complete English Poems, Penguin Classics, 1976)

Dostoevsky, Fyodor, *Crime and Punishment* (Wordsworth Editions, 2010)

Gaskell, Elizabeth, *The Life of Charlotte Brontë* (Penguin Classics, 1998)

Gibran, Kahlil, *The Prophet* (BN Publishing, 2009)

Goethe, Johann Wolfgang von, *Elective Affinities* (Penguin Classics, 1978)

Goldsmith, Oliver, *She Stoops to Conquer* (Dover Publications, 1991)

Hitchens, Christopher, *Hitch-22: A Memoir* (Atlantic Books, 2010)

Jung, Carl, *Modern Man in Search of a Soul* (Routledge Classics, 2001)

Keats, John, *Endymion* (Complete Poems of John Keats, Random House, 1994)

Lewis, C.S., *The Four Loves* (William Collins, 2012)

Springs of Indian Wisdom (S.N.M Publications, 1965)

Sewell, Anna, *Black Beauty* (Puffin, 2008)

Shakespeare, William, *Hamlet* (Wordsworth Editions, 1992)

Shakespeare, William, *Much Ado About Nothing* (Wordsworth Editions, 1995)

Shakespeare, William, *The Merry Wives of Windsor* (Wordsworth Editions, 1995)

Shelley, Mary, *Frankenstein* (Collins Classics, 2010)

Woolf, Virginia, *The Waves* (Wordsworth Editions, 2000)

Websites

www.integratedsociopyschology.net

www.fowler.uscd.edu

www.springer.com

Journals

Springer Journals

QUOTES ARE TAKEN FROM:

Albert Einstein was a theoretical physicist. He is renowned for developing the general theory of relativity and received the Nobel Prize for Physics in 1921.

Anna Sewell was an English writer who is best known for her book *Black Beauty*.

Aristotle is one of greatest philosophers from ancient Greece, his work has had a long-lasting influence on the development of all Western philosophical theories.

Arthur C. Clarke was a British science fiction writer most famous for co-writing the screenplay for the film *2001: A Space Odyssey*.

Benjamin Franklin was one of the Founding Fathers of the United States. He was a scientist, inventor, writer and diplomat and a major figure in the American Enlightenment.

Carl Jung was a revolutionary psychiatrist and psychotherapist. He is best known for having founded analytical psychology.

C.S. Lewis was one of the literary giants of the twentieth century. His most renowned books are *The Chronicles of Narnia* series and *The Screwtape Letters*.

Charles Darwin was an English naturalist and geologist who made significant contributions to science with his theories on evolution.

Charles Dickens was a Victorian novelist and social critic well-known for his books *A Christmas Carol*, *Oliver Twist* and *Great Expectations*.

Charlotte Brontë was the eldest of the three literary Brontë sisters. Her most renowned work is *Jane Eyre*.

Christopher Hitchens was a notorious author, journalist and debater who wrote *Hitch-22: A Memoir* and *Mortality*, the last of which he wrote whilst he was dying of cancer. Martin Amis described him as 'one of the most terrifying rhetoricians the world has seen.'

Dorothy Parker was an American writer and poet and founding member of the Algonquin Round Table. Her first collection of poetry, *Enough Rope*, was published in 1926 and was a bestseller.

Elbert Hubbard was an American writer and publisher.

Eleanor Roosevelt was an American politician and wife of President Franklin Roosevelt. She was the longest-serving First Lady of the United States.

Elizabeth Gaskell was a Victorian novelist, her famous works include *Cranford, North and South* and *The Life of Charlotte Brontë*.

Elizabeth J. Aries is a Professor in Social Sciences at Amherst College, Massachusetts.

Emily Brontë wrote only one book, but it is considered a seminal landmark in Gothic fiction, *Wuthering Heights*.

Emily Dickinson is considered to be one of the most important American poets of the nineteenth century and spent much of her life as a recluse.

Empedocles was an influential Greek philosopher who pre-dated Socrates, Plato and Aristotle. He is best known for his theory that all matter is made up of four elements; fire, air, water and earth.

Euripides was a famed tragedian of Classic Athens. He is believed to have written over 90 plays.

Frederich Nietzsche was a German philosopher in the nineteenth century who coined the phrase 'God is dead'.

Fyodor Dostoevsky was a Russian writer in the nineteenth century. His most renowned work *Crime and Punishment,* but his novella *Notes from the Underground* is widely considered to be one of the first works of extistentialist literature.

Helen Keller was an American author, who was born deaf-blind and became a symbol of courage across America.

Henry Ford was the the inventor of the model-T automobile.

Henry Thoreau was an American author and poet.

Hilaire Belloc was an Anglo-French historian and writer best known for his work *The Cautionary Tales for Children.*

Jane Austen was an English novelist well-known for her works of romantic fiction, including *Pride and Prejudice, Mansfield Park, Sense and Sensibility* and *Emma.*

Jim Morrison was the lead singer in the iconic band The Doors.

John Bunyan was an English preacher and author who wrote the famous Christian allegory *The Pilgrim's Progress.*

Johann Wolfgang von Goethe was a German poet, playwright and novelist and is considered the greatest German literary figure of the modern era.

John Donne was a leading metaphysical poet of the Renaissance and cleric in the Church of England. He is known for his love poetry and religious verse.

John Keats was a contemporary of Percy Shelley, and is considered to be one of the greatest English poets.

Kahlil Gibran was a Lebanese poet and writer. He is the third best-selling poet of all time and wrote *The Prophet* in 1926, which has never been out of print.

Katherine Mansfield is famous for her modernist short stories and also for her posthumously published journal.

Marcus Tullius Cicero is considered one of Rome's greatest orators and was a philosopher, politician and lawyer.

Mark Twain (Samuel Langhorne Clemens) was an American author who wrote the *The Adventures of Huckleberry Finn*, is often referred to as 'the great American novel'.

Marlene Dietrich was a screen goddess of the 1930s famed for her femme fatale roles in films such as *Morocco*.

Mary Shelley was a novelist and daughter of Mary Wollstonecraft, who was an advocate of women's rights. Shelley is best known for her novel *Frankenstein* which she wrote as part of a competition with Lord Byron, Percy Shelley and John Polidori to see who could write the best horror story.

Maya Angelou was an African-American author and poet. She was best known for her autobiographies, and most renowned was her first, *I Know Why the Caged Bird Sings*.

Muhammad Ali is a former American professional boxer.

Oliver Goldsmith was an Irish novelist and poet, who is best known for his novel *The Vicar of Wakefield*.

Oprah Winfrey is an American talk show host and is best known for her internationally renowned TV show *The Oprah Winfrey Show*.

Oscar Wilde was an Irish writer, playwright and poet. He is best known for his book *The Picture of Dorian Grey* and his play *The Importance of Being Earnest*.

Pythagoras was a Greek philosopher and mathmatician which the term Pythagoras's Theorem is named after.

Ralph Waldo Emerson was an American preacher, philosopher, lecturer and poet, and the leader of the Transcendentalist movement.

Robin Dunbar is an anthropologist and evolutionary psychologist. He was awarded the Huxley Memorial Medal in 2015 for services to anthropology.

Samuel Johnson was one of the most famous literary figures of the eighteenth century. His best-known work is his *Dictionary of the English Language.*

Swami Sivananda Saraswati was a famous Hindu spiritual teacher.

Virginia Woolf was an English writer in the twentieth century. Along with her husband she set up the Hogarth Press and also was a founding member of the famous Bloomsbury Group.

William Shakespeare was an English poet, actor and playwright. He is now considered one of the greatest writers in the English language and his works include, *Hamlet, Macbeth* and *King Lear.*

Woodrow Wilson was the 28th president of the United States and formed the League of Nations at The Treaty of Versailles.

Zadie Smith is a British novelist who was included on Granta's list of 20 best young authors in 2003 and 2013. In 2005 she won the Orange Prize for fiction. Her works include *White Teeth, On Beauty* and *The Autograph Man.*

PAGE REFERENCES

Page 11: Goethe, Johann Wolfgang von, *Elective Affinities* (Penguin classics, 1978)

Page 31: taken from *Hitch-22: A Memoir* by Christopher Hitchens, reproduced with kind permission of Atlantic Books Ltd.

Page 40: Reprinted with permission of HarperCollins Publishers Ltd. © 1968, Arthur C. Clarke

Page 41: www.integratedsociopsychology.net/Friendship_Development/'MyBestFriend'-BrianBigelow&JohnLaGaipa1.html based upon a study conducted by Bigelow in 1977 with a group of Scottish school children

Page 44–45: With kind permission from Springer Science+Business Media: Close Friendship in Adulthood: Conversational Content Between Same-Sex Friends, Sex Roles, Vol.9, 1983, No.12, Elizabeth J. Aries

Page 46: Reprinted with permission of Zadie Smith

Page 49: Reprinted with permission of The Guardian and The Observer Limited, London (March 2010)

Page 113: Angelou, Maya, Letters to my Daughter (Little Brown, 2012) permission granted by Little, Brown Book Group

Page 124: *The Four Loves* by C.S. Lewis © C.S. Lewis Pte Ltd 1960

Editorial director Anne Furniss
Creative director Helen Lewis
Editor Romilly Morgan
Editorial assistant Harriet Butt
Designers Emily Lapworth, Gemma Hogan
Production director Vincent Smith
Production controller Emily Noto

First published in 2014 by
Quadrille Publishing Ltd
52–54 Southwark Street,
London, SE1 1UN
www.quadrille.co.uk

Reprinted in 2014, 2016
10 9 8 7 6 5 4 3

British Library Cataloguing-in-Publication Data
A catalogue record for this book is available from the British Library.

ISBN: 978 184949 535 6

Printed in China